CONTENTS

HOW TO USE THE CD ACCOMPANIMENT:

THE CD IS PLAYABLE ON ANY CD PLAYER, AND IS ALSO ENHANCED SO MAC AND PC USERS CAN ADJUST THE RECORDING TO ANY TEMPO WITHOUT CHANGING THE PITCH.

A MELODY CUE APPEARS ON THE RIGHT CHANNEL ONLY. IF YOUR CD PLAYER HAS A BALANCE ADJUSTMENT, YOU CAN ADJUST THE VOLUME OF THE MELODY BY TURNING DOWN THE RIGHT CHANNEL.

ISBN 978-1-4234-6700-7

HAL•LEONARD®
CORPORATION
7777 W. BLUEMOUND RD. P.O. BOX 13819 MILWAUKEE, WI 53213

Visit Hal Leonard Online at
www.halleonard.com

◆1 ALL SHOOK UP

Words and Music by OTIS BLACKWELL
and ELVIS PRESLEY

CELLO

② BLUE SUEDE SHOES

Words and Music by
CARL LEE PERKINS

CELLO

❸ CAN'T HELP FALLING IN LOVE

CELLO

Words and Music by GEORGE DAVID WEISS,
HUGO PERETTI and LUIGI CREATORE

DON'T BE CRUEL
(To a Heart That's True)

CELLO

Words and Music by OTIS BLACKWELL
and ELVIS PRESLEY

◆ HOUND DOG

CELLO

Words and Music by JERRY LEIBER
and MIKE STOLLER

◆ I WANT YOU, I NEED YOU, I LOVE YOU

CELLO

Words and Music by MAURICE MYSELS
and IRA KOSLOFF

♦ 7 IT'S NOW OR NEVER

CELLO

Words and Music by AARON SCHROEDER
and WALLY GOLD

JAILHOUSE ROCK

CELLO

Words and Music by JERRY LEIBER
and MIKE STOLLER

♦⑨ LOVE ME

CELLO

Words and Music by JERRY LEIBER
and MIKE STOLLER

◆ LOVE ME TENDER

CELLO

Words and Music by ELVIS PRESLEY
and VERA MATSON

◆ LOVING YOU

CELLO

Words and Music by JERRY LEIBER
and MIKE STOLLER

⬦12 RETURN TO SENDER

CELLO

Words and Music by OTIS BLACKWELL
and WINFIELD SCOTT

◆13 (LET ME BE YOUR) TEDDY BEAR

CELLO

Words and Music by KAL MANN
and BERNIE LOWE

◆14 TOO MUCH

Words and Music by LEE ROSENBERG
and BERNARD WEINMAN

CELLO

WEAR MY RING AROUND YOUR NECK

CELLO

Words and Music by BERT CARROLL
and RUSSELL MOODY